Compiled by Geng Mo

CHINESE CLOTH ART

CHINA INTERCONTINENTAL PRESS

图书在版编目（CIP）数据

中国布艺：英文／耿默编著；严马，王国振译.—北京：五洲传播出版社，2007.12
（中国民间工艺品丛书）
ISBN 978-7-5085-1208-2

Ⅰ.中…　Ⅱ.①耿…②严…③王…　Ⅲ.布料－工艺美术－简介－中国－英文
Ⅳ.J529

中国版本图书馆 CIP 数据核字（2007）第 171796 号

策　　划：荆孝敏
编　　著：耿　默
翻　　译：严　马　王国振
责任编辑：王　莉
装帧设计：缪　惟　汪俊宇

中国布艺

出版发行：五洲传播出版社
社　　址：北京市海淀区莲花池东路北小马厂 6 号华天大厦
邮政编码：100038
电　　话：010-58891281
传　　真：010-58891281
制版单位：北京锦绣圣艺文化发展有限公司
印　　刷：北京郎翔印刷有限公司
开　　本：889x1194　1/24
印　　张：4.5
版　　次：2008 年 10 月第 2 版　2008 年 10 月第 1 次印刷
书　　号：ISBN 978-7-5085-1208-2
定　　价：68.00 元

Preface

The cloth art of China refers to cloth handicrafts made by Chinese people using traditional cloth and threads as raw materials. These are tailored, sewn and adorn the different cloths. Cloth handicrafts come in such forms as embroidery, Gesi tapestry, hand stitching, embroidery paste, barbola, brocade and batik.

Chinese people were the first to raise silkworms and from the cocoons they made silk thread which was used to weave silk fabrics. Yuanfei, the concubine of the Yellow Emperor, personally raised silkworms and called on all other women to do likewise. The emperor himself personally took part in tilling and popularized silkworm raising technology among the people. In this way a traditional system was introduced for the raising of silkworms. This, plus the system introduced some 4,000 years ago for people of different social strata to wear garments with different colours and designs, prompted the fast development of the weaving and embroidering technologies in China. Using only needle and thread the Chinese quickly learned to make decorative garments. This helped to make peoples lives more colourful and satisfied the people's need for a better quality of life. This, in turn, contributed to the development of civilization in China.

Embroidering, which originated as silk embroidering, is done mostly by women. It is now called Nuhong or needlecraft. As the art was passed down historically between mother and daughter, or between the mother-in-law and the daughter-in-law, it became known as the "mother's art." Chinese cloth art found great popularity with the tribal groups and families for thousands of years and retains the most primitive art form of ancient China. It also reflects ancient Chinese worship and beliefs. Cloth art includes garments, toys and articles for daily use. Cloth art helps relieve the boredom of everyday life by making everyday items more colourful. It reminds the people of their history and customs through the designs and thus helps retain their individuality.

In early times in China the standard of living was primitive and the most important things were survival and procreation.

Nature changed so quickly and mysteriously that the people imagined there was a supernatural force that existed behind the changes. This lent support to their imagination that "each figure or pattern had a meaning and the meaning must be auspicious." Gradually the people created drawings of their ancestors, lucky animals, flowers, plants, geometric lines and other patterns to bring good luck and avoid evil.

While making hats, shoes and dresses as well as a variety of pillows and cloth toys in the shape of divine beings, women always adorned them with the pattern of "A Tiger" or "A Tiger Who Suppresses the Five Poisonous Creatures" (referring to scorpions, snakes, centipedes, geckos and toads). The purpose was to pray for good luck to dispel the evil so that the children would grow up healthy. Belts, Hebao bags, pillows and other dowry items were all adorned with such patterns as "Mandarin Ducks Playing in Water," "Lotus Bidding for Sons," and "Carp Swimming Among the Lotus Plants." They represent good wishes for a happy marriage and "The More the Sons the Happier the Life." Articles presented to old people often carry patterns symbolizing "happiness, fortune and long life." Other patterns include bats, deer and long life peaches to wish good health, more children and a healthy life. All these patterns that depict hope show how much the people believed that appeasing the Gods was essential in order to have a good and happy life.

Embroidery is the most popular method used in cloth art. There are many different embroidery styles and schools. The major ones include Suzhou embroidery, Guangdong embroidery, Sichuan embroidery and Hunan embroidery and these are the most famous in China.

A close look at the cloth art of China shows that the family concept is the basis no matter how much society changed. The cloth art of China has passed down the history of China no matter what the conditions were. In particular and importantly it contains the folk culture of the different ethnic groups.

【CONTENTS】

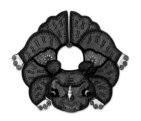

Children's Hats

Children's hats are used to protect the children from the different elements the sun, wind and rain, also to keep them warm. However, they also show the peoples religion and are used by the old to give good wishes to the young. Out of their love for their children, women display their creativity to create numerous kinds of children's hats.

In northern China and some parts of southern China, children's hats decorated with the pattern of a tiger's or lion's head are the most common. This is because tigers and lions are thought of as kings of animals and the people hope they will help protect them. As most of the women have never had a chance to see a real tiger or lion what they do is create these animals according to what they are told. With the lapse of time the images of the tigers and the lions used to adorn the children's hats became similar all over.

Hats for boys include those having the shape of a whole tiger, a tiger with two heads, a whole lion, a lion with two heads, a unicorn, a butterfly flying around lotus flowers or fish swimming among lotus flowers.

Hats for girls include those having the shape of a lotus, marrow squash, pomegranate, or a phoenix.

All the hats are embroidered and decorated with hanging threads and silver or bronze bells. The people believe the sound from the silver or bronze bells will scare away the evil spirits and thus protect the children.

In areas in southern China, where the ethnic minorities live in compact communities, ancient hats for children that can still be found are mostly those found among the children of the Dong and Miao ethnic groups. They are embroidered with patterns such as the dragon or the phoenix, two dragons playing with a pearl, and butterflies and these are also adorned with silver or bronze chips. Some of these hats are decorated with a silver pattern of "Avalokitesvara Giving Blessings to the Children."

A Tiger's Head Hat

Most of the folk hats found today are tiger-head hats. People make tiger-head hats as a token of worship to the fierce and holy animal and also to get protection from it. The picture shows a tiger-head hat for a child from shanxi province.

A Tiger's Head Hat

This child's hat comes from Anhui Province. The green satin cloth printed with patterns is decorated with a tiger's head and the body of the animal is sewn using gold thread.

A Decorative Part of a Child's Hat

This is the decorative part of a child's hat popular among the people of Shanxi Province. This style of decorative piece is often attached to hats worn in winter. The scene embroidered here is a street scene.

A Decorative Part of a Child's Hat

This also comes from Shanxi Province and is embroidered also with a street scene. It forms a pair with the above piece.

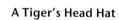

A Tiger's Head Hat

This hat, found in the southern part of Shanxi Province, was made following a design created according to the age of the children and the changing seasons. These hats are elegant in shape and the colours are very bright. They also need good embroidery art. The "ears," the "eyes" and the "tongues" of such hats can sway with movement.

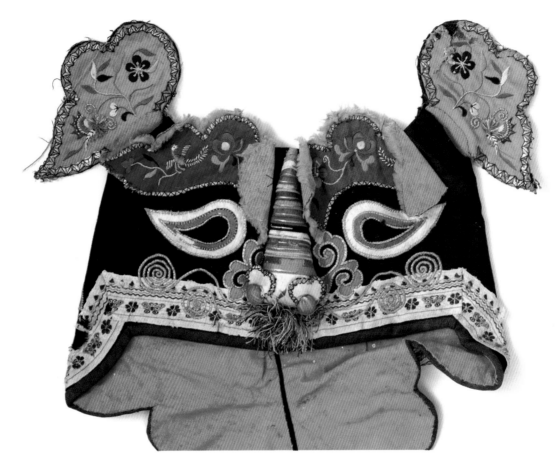

A Lion's and Tiger's Head Hat

This hat again from the southern part of Shanxi Province features a combination design of both the lion's and tiger's heads.

A Tiger's Head Hat

This hat, another from the southern part of Shanxi Province, features rich and harmonious colours which come from the use of the sequin embroidery method.

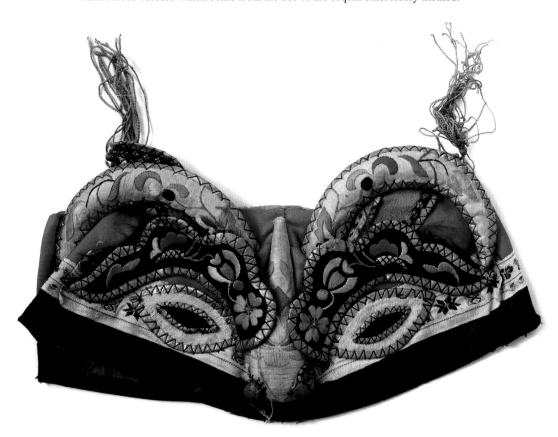

A Tiger's Head Hat

    This hat, unique to Jiangsu Province, features a black background. It was made using the barbola and inlay art to highlight the five organs of the tiger. Its two ears are decorated with two dangling embroidered balls.

A Tiger Hat

This hat comes from the Dingxiang region of Shanxi Province. It has the shape of a complete tiger.

A Child's Hat of the Dong Ethnic Group

This hat comes from the Rongjiang Dong ethnic group area of Guizhou Province. It is embroidered with a pattern of two dragons playing a pearl. This pattern is one of the most well known in China.

A Child's Hat of the Dong Ethnic Group

This hat also comes from the Rongjiang Dong ethnic group area of Guizhou
Province. The top is embroidered with a dragon pattern and small pieces of
silver are added to depict "Avalokitesvara Giving Blessings to the Children."

A Child's Hat of the Miao Ethnic Group

This hat comes from the Rongjiang Miao ethnic group area of Guizhou Province. The hat top is embroidered with such patterns as butterflies, peonies and fish to symbolize life.

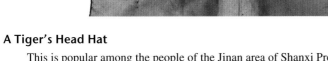

A Tiger's Head Hat

This is popular among the people of the Jinan area of Shanxi Province. Embroidered in the high relief barbola method, this child's hat is decorated with an awesome looking tigers head.

A Decorative Part of a Child's Hat

This is the decorative part of a child's hat. There is an old Chinese saying, "Good things happen when a lion rolls an embroidered ball." The design of the "Lion Rolling an Embroidered Ball" is therefore used to decorate the rear part of the hat. This hat comes from Shanxi Province.

A Decorative Part of a Child's Hat

This is the decorative part of a child's hat, also coming from Shanxi Province, has good luck patterns meaning riches, happiness, long life and good luck.

Cloth Toys

Many cloth toys take the form of a tiger, a lion, a dragon, a phoenix, a chicken or a fish which people of the older generation love because of the stories behind them. They are meant to portray "Liveliness and Energy," "Good Luck" and "Riches and Glamour."

The Chinese have worshipped the tiger since ancient times. This worship began in the time of Nu Wa (the Goddess of Sky Patching) and Fu Xi or Fu Hsi (who was the first of the mythical Three Sovereigns in ancient China). In June 1987 some ruins of the Yangshao Culture some 6,000 years ago was found in Puyang, Henan Province. They included a large tomb for a male in which was found some clam shells with dragon and tiger carvings on them. This was the first time such shell carvings had been found and they show that even in primitive China the people worshipped the tiger and the dragon. This proves that the dragon and tiger worship culture has existed for a long time. Eventually this culture found its way into the design and shape of toys.

The people think tigers are holy and they protect them in life. This is why tigers are used as the most popular form for children's toys. The people hope that the tiger will protect the children from evil spirits.

Cloth tiger toys come with a lot of variations. They are popular in the areas drained by the Yellow, Yangtze and Huaihe Rivers. Very often women make cloth tiger pillow toys, hence the name of "tiger pillows" which are very popular amongst the peasants. Generally, a cloth tiger pillow measures one-third of a metre. Such pillows are used by children as toys during the day and as pillows at night. With the protection of the tigers the children are kept away from evil and sleep soundly.

A Cloth Tiger Pillow

This one is made in Anhui Province and is a typical tiger headed pillow. The shape of this pillow shows it was made from a practical point. It is pleasing to the eye and comfortable.

A Snakenosed Tiger Pillow

This one was made in Shanxi Province. The snake-shaped nose of the tiger is embroidered with symmetrical fish. This design is an original historical one which depicts that the two gods, the dragon and the tiger, can coexist together. This idea came from our ancient primitive society where it was first used as an artwork design.

A Cloth Tiger Pillow

This one was made in Henan Province. In shaping this tiger more attention is paid to its practical use. The tiger head, held high, is connected with the outspread body and finished with its tail curling upwards. The span from beginning to end may just protect the head of the child while sleeping on it.

A Cloth Tiger Pillow

This one was made in Henan Province. In depicting this tiger more attention was paid to its ornamental and play uses. The tiger's legs are stretched ready to jump or run.

A Dragon Tiger Pillow

    This one was made in Shanxi Province. The tail of the tiger is snake-shaped and there are outstanding snake heads on both sides of the tiger. It is a combination of a tiger and a snake showing that the two gods, the dragon and the tiger, coexist in folk artwork.

A Cloth Tiger Pillow

This one was made in Shaanxi Province. The embroidery of Shaanxi Province is vigorous and firm in shape and features sculptures dating back to the Qin (221BC-206BC) and Han (206BC-220AD) Dynasties. This cloth tiger, wearing a corolla on its head, is twined with wool balls of various colours. From a visual point of view this one is for a girl.

A Frog's Body and Tiger's Head Pillow

This one was made in Shanxi Province. This tiger's head and frog's body toy is very suitable for a baby.

A Cloth Tiger Pillow

This one was made in Shanxi Province. In this design the tiger is wearing an official hat and is entwined by five poisonous creatures. This design has the wish that the child using the pillow will be immune to poisons and have a successful career as an official.

A Tiger's Head and Fish Tail Pillow

This tiger pillow is popular in Shanxi Province. This tiger's head and fish tail pillow is embroidered with two symmetrical fish at each side of the body which through *Yin* and *Yang* directly implies intercourse and in turn the continuation of the race.

A Cloth Tiger Pillow

This toy, made in Henan Province, is a typical folk tiger pillow. The author shaped this work into a tiger cub. While depicting the lovely and babyish image of the little tiger she also paid attention to its practical use.

Cloth Lion Pillows

The pair of cloth pillows were made in Jiangsu Province. The lion-shaped pillows resemble a little the images of dancing lions found in the south of the lower reaches of the Yangtze River.

The Ear Pillow

The ear pillow is a practical work of art which is very popular in northwest China. As well as being practical (for sleeping on) it makes a good ornament (as a cushion) and can be used as a toy by the children.

Generally the ear pillow is made in the shape of a frog or a fish. The centre is made hollow usually with the design of a flower or the sun. It is specially designed by mothers to prevent their children's ears from being hurt when they lie on their side to sleep. Beautiful patterns are embroidered on the ear pillows. Most of them are of a fish, frog or tortoise, which were regarded as the origins of man by the ancestors of the people in northwest China in ancient times. These symbols also have the meaning of having many children and long life.

Besides the main patterns of fish, frog and tortoise, the patterns of the sun and stars are also embroidered on the frog or fish-shaped ear pillows. The latter represents the constellations at night and the bright sky during the day. Some ear pillows are embroidered with natural items such as lotus flowers, peonies, butterflies and the five poisonous creatures which symbolize in turn riches, honour, good luck and warding off evil. Chinese herbal medicine is sometimes placed in the ear pillow and helps keep away mosquitoes and aids the child's health. This shows a mothers love combined with the ingenuity of traditional Chinese medicine.

A Fish-Shaped Ear Pillow

This ear pillow, made in Gansu Province, is in the shape of a fish. The body of the fish is embroidered with an outstanding frog on which the stars are embroidered. This is a symbol of male offspring.

A Frog-Shaped Ear Pillow

This ear pillow, made in Gansu Province, is in the shape of a frog. Its centre is embroidered with the sun which is surrounded by stars, symbolizing the intercourse of heaven and earth and the circle of life.

An Ear Pillow

This ear pillow was made in Gansu Province. Its shape is common, but its entire design is very unique. Its centre is embroidered with a beautiful carp with a hole in the body.

A Fish-Shaped Ear Pillow

This ear pillow, made in Gansu Province, is in the shape of a fish. The body of the fish is made from gold thread and the tail is embroidered with a peony symbolizing wealth and rank.

An Ear Pillow

    This ear pillow was made in Gansu Province. The pattern in the centre is composed of two fish intersecting at the tail on lotus flowers. This symbolizes having many children and having a surplus crop in successive years.

A Frog-Shaped Ear Pillow

This ear pillow, made in Gansu Province, is in the shape of a frog. In the centre is a fish flanked by a pair of embroidered ducks. This is a symbol of having many sons.

A Fish-Shaped Ear Pillow

This ear pillow, made in Gansu Province, is in the shape of a beautiful fish. A lotus flower in full blossom is embroidered where the hollow is made in the centre. This is a symbol of having a surplus of crops in successive years.

A Frog-Shaped Ear Pillow

This ear pillow, made in Shaanxi Province, is in the shape a frog and on which a large scorpion is embroidered. This implies that the child will not be afraid of the "five poisonous creatures" and will be immune to poisons and have good health.

A Tortoise-Shaped Ear Pillow

 This ear pillow, made in Shanxi Province, is in the shape of a tortoise. It is embroidered with lucky flowers which are representing long life, wealth and high rank.

Traditional Baby Bibs

A baby's bib is a piece of cloth which is secured under the chin to protect the clothing from being dirtied by the baby if it dribbles while eating. In this sense it is a very practical item. In the past a bib was generally given as a present by the grandparents to the baby when they were a month old, 100 days old or a year old.

The material chosen for the bib is normally very soft. They are comfortable to wear and look beautiful. The implied meaning in giving the bib is usually good luck and good health.

The patterns embroidered on the bibs include a cherub wishing the child healthy growth. The pomegranate, peony and peach represent the fact that the more sons the more blessings and long life. Tigers have the meaning of warding off evil spirits and enjoying a life of ease and comfort. The bibs embroidered with the patterns of the "Twin Tigers With One Head," the "Twin Lions With One Head" and the "Five Happiness Holding Longevity" are suitable for a baby boy, while those with the patterns of the "Five Butterflies Holding Flowers," the "Baby Sitting on the Lotus Flower" and the "Five Fish Playing Between the Lotus Leaves" for a baby girl.

A Ruyi Bib

The shape of this bib is four *Ruyis* (an S-shaped ornamental object usually made from jade symbolizing good luck) each one embroidered with two pairs of symmetrical bats and peonies in the centre. The meaning implied in Chinese means: "May you have all your wishes and hopes come true." This pertains particularly to wealth and honour.

A "Twin Lions With One Head" Bib

This pattern indicates that the two lions have the same head.

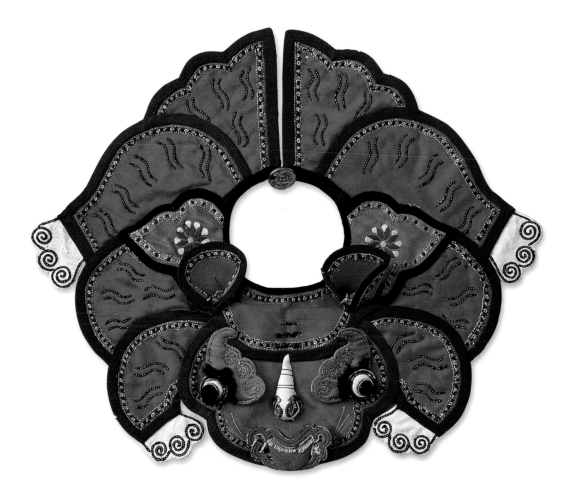

A "Twin Tigers With One Head" Bib

This pattern indicates that the two tigers have the same head.

An "Eight Lucky Treasures" Bib

The pattern on the upper part of this bib is the "Eight Lucky Treasures" while on the lower part of it is the "Happy News on Life." The "Eight Lucky Treasures," also known as the "Eight Lucky Symbols" and as the "Miscellaneous Treasures," is a combination of the "Properties of the Eight Immortals" which are the wheel, conch, umbrella, lid, flower, bottle, goldfish and Panchang sausages. It is a design commonly used for embroidery patterns.

A "Fish Darting and Playing Between the Lotus Leaves" Bib

The pattern embroidered on the centre of this bib is a big carp and a full bloom lotus flower. The bib with this pattern is usually for a baby girl and is a symbol of family growth and wishes for many children.

Traditional Hebao Bags

The predecessor of the Hebao bag is called "He Nang" in Chinese. The Chinese character "He" refers to a lotus flower in the dictionary and it also has the meaning of burden. People in many parts of China have long been used to wrapping things in lotus leaves. With the development of needlecraft the old custom gradually evolved into the handcraft "Hebao bags."

There are also many terms in Chinese for the Hebao bag such as "fragrant bag" and "accessory bag" and includes purse.

The custom of carrying Hebao bags began in the Eastern Zhou Dynasty (770 BC-256 BC) and continued through the Tang (618-907), Song (960-1279), Yuan (1206-1368), Ming (1368-1644) and Qing (1644-1911) Dynasties and the early Republic of China. In feudal times Hebao bags were a necessary part of imperial apparel and used daily by the majority of the people.

The Hebao bags in old times served many purposes and showed a persons status. They were also sent as gifts on festive occasions. They were also regarded as a pledge of love and a gift for marriage as well as an accessory carried for warding off the five poisonous creatures. Due to the diversity of folk customs Hebao bags have different shapes for daily use such as elliptical, square, guava, peach, gourd and S-shaped. The manner in which they are used also vary such as a shoulder bag, a belly bag, a fragrant bag, a purse, a cigarette bag and various other ways. With respect to making them some are made from Gesi tapestry or brocade, some are painted and stitched with various decorative designs and embossed brocade. In particular the hand embroidered Hebao bags are the most valuable and are regarded as one of the best among the traditional embroideries.

The Palace Lantern Hebao Bag

   This one belongs to the late Qing Dynasty (1644-1911) and is in the shape of a palace lantern which is very rare among Hebao bags. It has many stitching techniques such as pigtail-style embroidery, winding embroidery, knot embroidery and couching embroidery with gold foil wrapping the border. The manner in which this bag is made shows that it was not made for a common person. There is a musical instrument, a chess set, paintings, a persimmon, a *Ruyi* (an S-shaped ornamental object usually made from jade symbolizing good luck) and a coin embroidered on it. The peony, a symbol of riches and honour, embroidered in the centre suggests the theme of this Hebao bag.

A Belly Hebao Bag

The decorative pattern is "Continuously Giving Birth to Child." The Pure Land Sect (also called the Lotus Sect) of Chinese Buddhism has a picture entitled the "Western Paradise" in which a peaceful vision appears. In this vision people have ample food and clothing, are singing and dancing in celebration of good times and babies sit cheerfully on lotus flowers. In folk embroidery and New Year pictures there is also a design of a boy holding a lotus flower or a jade musical instrument sheng sitting on a lotus flower. It symbolizes many children.

A Belly Hebao Bag

The decorative pattern here is a "Lion Rolling Embroidered Balls." The lion was introduced to China in the Han Dynasty (206 BC-220 AD) and is considered a lucky animal. As early as the Tang Dynasty (618-907) there was a design of "A Pair of Lions Playing With a Ball" which is a lucky sign.

A Square Hebao Bag

The decorative pattern is "The Two Immortals" and these are the happy immortals in folklore. Originally there was one immortal and later it evolved into two. They both have virtue and wisdom and are content with their lot. This embroidery wishes harmony and happiness. The two immortals are also known as the "Two Sages."

A Shoulder Bag

The decorative pattern is "Continuously Giving Birth to Child." The shoulder bag is used by both men and women and is stuck into the waistband. This is another safe way to carry money and valuables. The shape is rectangular with a bag at each end and the design is usually the same on each bag with, perhaps, some variation but the meaning should be the same.

A Shoulder Bag

The decorative pattern is "Lying on the Ice Looking for Carp" above and "Mu Guiying Becomes the Chief General" below which are two traditional operas.

A Purse Cover

The decorative pattern is "The Legend of the White Snake" which became an opera after being rewritten from folklore. The scene embroidered on it is like this: During the Dragon Boat Festival, Xu Xian brought real liquor and persuaded his wife (the White Snake) to drink again and again. After drinking the liquor she changed back into her original shape which frightened Xu Xian to death.

A Unique Hebao bag

The decorative pattern here is "A Bittern Sleeping on a Lotus Flower" which implies the multiplying of life. The bird lays its eggs in order to have more birds and this continues in an endless succession. The lotus flower, lotus seed pod and lotus seed means continuation this combination symbolizes continuous offspring.

A Flower Basket-Shaped Hebao Bag

The decorative pattern is "The Revolt of the Fishing People" which is a traditional opera. The scene embroidered on it goes like this: Xiao' en and his daughter are sitting on boat and a Qing Dynasty (1644-1911) official is standing on the bank and collecting taxes forcibly. This flower basket-shaped Hebao bag features the shape of a common flower basket. This bag can be separated into smaller parts which is ideal for carrying small items which should be kept apart.

A Square Hebao bag

The decorative pattern is the "Memorial at the Pagoda," which is also called "Si-lam Offering a Sacrifice in the Leifangta Pagoda" which is an excerpt from the opera *The Legend of the White Snake*. The scene embroidered on it goes like this: The White Snake is kept under the Leifangta Pagoda by Monk Fatt Hoi. The son of the White Snake called Shilin won a competition for the Number One Scholar. Given directions by immortals he went to the Leifangta Pagoda to offer a sacrifice to his mother.

A Belly Hebao Bag

The decorative pattern here is "Hunting in the Garden" which is also called "The Rabbit Jumping Into the Garden." These are highlights chosen from a traditional opera entitled "Zhao Kuangyin and Zheng'en Beating the Iron-arm King in the Palace." Prime Minister Fu Qi has two daughters, the elder being Empress Wang and the younger called Fu Lanying who has been betrothed to the son of Han Tong named Han Luoguo. Fu had a dream one night that a jackal grabbed a gold hair pin but it was taken back by a blue dragon. She and her maid went to the garden to burn incense. At the same time Zhao Kuangyi, the younger brother of Zhao Kuangyin, went out hunting with Miao Xun. Zhao fired an arrow at a white rabbit but it escaped with the arrow in its mouth. Zhao chased it into a garden and saw it ran to Fu Lanying. Zhao and Fu met and fell in love with each other and lived happily ever after.

A Drum-Shaped Hebao Bag

The decorative pattern is "Fighting Against Lubu" which is a local traditional opera. The drum-shaped Hebao bag is in the shape of an oblate bass drum. This style of bag is usually given as a gift especially at weddings.

A Square Purse

The decorative pattern is called "Plucking Osmanthus Blossoms From the Moon." It originally referred to the method of selecting talented people. Later, people used it to describe the people passing the palace examination and the people having a prosperous official career. In the myth there are osmanthus in the palace of the moon so the pattern has the moral that one has been entitled to as a high-ranking official. The deer, which has a partial tone with the word salary in the Chinese language, in the pattern implies the character in the pattern being entitled to a position as a high-ranking official. In addition, the official clothes on the central character also imply it.

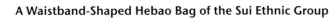

A Waistband-Shaped Hebao Bag of the Sui Ethnic Group

    The decorative pattern here is a fish at the top, a deer in the middle and a dragon on the bottom.

Square Hebao Bag

    The decorative pattern is called "The Unicorn Brings the Child," also known as "A Newborn Baby Brought by the Fairy." The unicorn is a lucky animal in ancient legend next only to the dragon in terms of the status among animals. It is a symbol of luck and can bring people babies.

A Square Hebao Bag

The decorative pattern here is "The Palace of Brahmā" a traditional opera. The scene embroidered on it goes like this: Liu Fu a Buddhist monk celebrates his birthday in the Palace of Brahmā. His daughter Xuemei, together with her husband Han Mei and Huayun her son, went to extend birthday congratulations. On the way Huayun shot down a wild goose.

A Square Purse

The decorative pattern is the "Legend of Lin Daiyu" one of the most moving scenes from the novel *A Dream of Red Mansions*. This particular part of the story was later transformed into local opera in different localities. The scene goes like this: Lin visited Baoyu at night but was refused entry by a maid with an evil tongue outside the door. Lin thought it was Baoyu who didn't meet her on purpose so she was very annoyed. The next day Daiyu saw the flowers on the ground and buried them and wrote a poem called the "Burial of Flowers," to try to get rid of her sadness. Luckily Baoyu came there and explained to her what had happened and then they became reconciled. People often embroider this kind of scene on a Hebao bag of love to express their yearning for a happy marriage.

A Belly Hebao Bag of the Dong Ethnic Group

The decorative pattern is "A Fish Turning Into a Dragon" and is also called "The Carp Jumps Over the Dragon Gate." This is one of the traditional lucky designs. In the pattern the head of the fish has already passed over the dragon gate and changed into that of a dragon leaving the tail of the fish in the air. It implies that a change of status brings a rise in luck.

A Belly Hebao Bag of the Sui Ethnic Group

　　The decorative pattern is a fish and boy flowers at the top and a phoenix and boy flowers on the bottom. A boy flower is a lucky flower in the eyes of the Miao, Dong and Sui ethnic groups. It is comprised of four butterflies of different designs. The four heads of flowers symbolize the four directions implying that people will be lucky and safe anywhere.

Pillow End Embroidery

The "pillow end embroidery" is one of the many Chinese embroidery varieties. It can be dated back to the period of the Western Han Dynasty (206BC-25AD) judging from the preserved examples that exist and became very popular in the later Qing Dynasty (1644-1911).

Generally the embroidered pillows popular among the ordinary people to this day are the rectangular ones. The two ends of the pillow are called the pillow end. The pillow end may be shaped in a square, a rectangle, a round or an ellipse. Pillow ends are usually embroidered with good luck patterns.

In old times pillow end embroidery was an important way of showing women's needlework craft. Girls were required to embroider the pillow ends under the guidance of the older women prior to marriage. In a way this was a form of needlework apprenticeship. Some girls made dozens or hundreds of pillow ends before they married. Of these embroidered pillow ends, apart from several pairs left as part of the dowry, the rest would be presented to friends and relatives according to the local customs.

The pattern themes on the pillow ends are very cultured. For example when congratulating newlyweds on their happy occasion their friends and relatives give them pillows with patterns such as "Fish Swimming Among the Lotus flowers," "A Dragon Playing With a Phoenix," "A Phoenix Playing With a Peony," "A Butterfly Loving a Flower" all of which are symbols of a happy love life. Alternatively they may be presented with pillows bearing the designs of a "Baby Sitting on Lotus Leaves," "Kylin Carrying a Son" and a "Fairy Bringing a Son" which implies the wishes for the couple to have many children. For older people's birthdays the design should be one which wishes them happiness and long life such as the "Pine Crane Belaying the Year"and "Bliss, Wealth, Longevity and Happiness." When congratulating young people on their birthdays people should give pillows with patterns such as the "Five Sons Passing the Imperial Examination," "Succeeding in a Government Examination," "Coming First in the Civil Service Examination in Former Times" and a "Lion Rolling an Embroidered Ball" as a present to show their encouragement.

The embroidered pillow end serves as part of their bedding and also as a beautiful ornament. The different patterns on the pillow ends also show the Chinese traditional custom of praying for blessings.

A Pillow End

  The pattern on this pillow end is entitled "Enjoying Riches and Honour for Life, and Having a Son." This pattern is made by using the tone and implied meaning of embroidered objects. A blooming peony is inserted into a bottle which has the implied meaning of "enjoying riches and honour for life." On the peony between two magpies is sitting a newly-born baby boy which symbolizes "having a son." The pattern directly expresses the implied meaning.

A Pillow End

The pattern on this pillow end is a "Baby Sitting on Lotus Flowers," expressing the good wishes of the giver for "bearing many sons and may they be always safe and sound."

A Pillow End

The pattern on this pillow end is the "Spring Ploughing Picture," depicting a rural scene in which a farmer is driving his ox to plough. In the pattern, the magpies are singing on the branches, the flowers are in bloom and leaves flourishing which represents a lucky atmosphere.

A Rectangle Pillow End

The pattern on this pillow end is the "Mandarin Ducks on a Lotus Leaf" with the implied meaning of increasing ones family. In China the mandarin ducks are a symbol of love. The lotus flower, lotus seed pod and lotus seed has the meaning of stretching long and unbroken. The combination of the two things symbolizes having a son and heir stretching long and unbroken i.e. never ending.

A Square Pillow End

   The pattern on this pillow end is the "Kylin Carrying a Son." The Kylin is a kind of good luck beast in ancient Chinese folklore. Among the animals its position is only second to the dragon. The Kylin, a symbol of good luck, may bring a son to human beings. People think of the mythical animal as having the shape of a deer's body with a single horn and have a habit of calling a very smart child a "Kylin."

A Square Pillow End

The pattern on this pillow end is the "Success in a Government Examination." In China's feudal society the final imperial examination is the highest one under the imperial examination system. The names of the successful candidates were written on yellow paper. This brought about the design of a golden billboard with the names on it which gives the title of "Official Post." The billboard is stamped with the great seal of the Emperor, i.e., "Treasure of the Emperor." The pattern of "Succeeding in a Government Examination" is a symbol of the young people achieving success and winning recognition.

A Square Pillow End

The pattern on this pillow end is the "Fairy Sending a Son." In old times a married woman went to the temple under the guidance of the senior women of the family and paid homage to the god and Buddha for the birth of a son. Legend has it that the god administering the birth of sons is "The Goddess Administering Birth" also known as "The Goddess Sending a Son" or the "Fairy Sending a Son." This kind of pillow end is given as a present to a newly married couple and has the implied meaning of having a son and heir continuing unbroken in the family.

A Square Pillow End

The pattern on this pillow end is the "Kylin Carrying a Son." This Kylin, in an imperial yellow robe, is followed by two waiters which symbolizes the birth of a son.

A Round Pillow End

The pattern on this pillow end is the "Tiger Putting Down Five Poisonous Creatures." The tiger is known as the "emperor of mountain animals" and the "king of the animals." In the "Annotation of Literature and Customs" it is written that the "tiger, a *Yang* thing, is the head of the animals." The tiger is regarded as a holy beast among the people and, due to its power to put down ghosts, wards off evil spirits and offers protection and safety.

Traditional Bellybands

Bellybands were traditional underwear popular in the royal court and among the people. Even today the custom remains of making bellybands in some areas of China.

Bellybands are mostly made by embroidery. Sometimes the method of sticking pieces of material together or a patching pattern is used. According to custom, women made the bellyband only for their lover, husband or children. Therefore, the patterns symbolizing good luck, love and having many children are the most commonly found.

Bellybands for women are made from monochromatic cloth (red), decorated with a little lacework and simple patterns. The patterns on the bellybands that they embroider for their lovers can come from many different sources but always have love as their theme. The most common ones found are those love stories taken from operas, myths and folklore.

The bellybands used as part of a dowry may have the "Prosperity Brought by the Dragon and the Phoenix," the "Fish Darting and Playing Between Lotus Leaves," the "Twin Lotus Flowers on One Stalk," the "Butterfly Loving a Flower," "Mandarin Ducks Playing in the Water," the "Phoenix Playing With a Peony" or a love story from an opera as the main pattern. These patterns convey the message for a new family starting a new life.

The patterns used for the bellybands embroidered for newly-born babies are mainly of the tiger for example the "Tiger Putting Down Five Poisonous Creatures" and "Bearing Many Sons." This directly expresses blessings for a new life and protection.

A Bellyband

The pattern on this bellyband is the "Lion Rolling an Embroidered Ball." Such patterns are specially designed for a baby boy and indicate wishes that the child will have a bright future.

A Bellyband

This bellyband was made in the area of Gaoping City, Shanxi Province. The pattern on it is the "White Rabbit and Fuwa" which is a symbol of life and many children. Bellybands made in Gaoping City, Shanxi Province belong to the patched embroidery style but they have their own unique style.

A Bellyband

    This is part of a bellyband made in Gaoping City, Shanxi Province. The patter on it is the "Record of a Journey to the West." The five sense organs cannot be seen on the faces of the characters in this picture and this is a characteristic of Gaoping embroidery. Restricted by the patchwork embroidery Gaoping embroidery generally uses the handmade method to embroider the faces of the characters on the bellyband or does not embroider at all.

A Bellyband

The pattern on this bellyband depicts the scene of a traditional opera entitled "Going Hunting in the Garden" which is also known as "The Rabbit Jumping Into a Garden" and which is a love play. The plot is that while chasing after a white rabbit, Zhao Kuangyin, the first emperor of the Song Dynasty (960-1279) enters into a garden. The white rabbit, which has his arrow in its mouth, runs up to Fu Lanying so Zhang and Fu meet, fall in love with each other and secretly plan their future life together.

A Bellyband

    The central pattern on this bellyband depicts a passage from a traditional opera. The edge of the bellyband is made from symmetrically printed cloth with different colours and the two lotus flowers on the upper and lower part of the collar band set off each other. This signifies a happy and harmonious love life.

Ethnic Embroidered Clothing

Clothing is the main platform for displaying ethnic embroidery. These embroidered patterns with harmonic colour arrangements and exquisite and fine embroidering skill are not only of good practical use, but of ornamental use and high artistic value. Ethnic embroidered clothing is most beautiful of all of China's ethnic products. It is a living fossil which can be used to trace the customs, cultural etiquette, art and history of all of China's ethnic groups.

Embroidery is widely popular among all the various ethnic groups. It is an important means for China's women to beautify their lives. It is also an important way of exchanging gifts between friends, neighbours and relatives for festivals and/or holidays. It is a very important part of wedding ceremonies and funeral rites.

The patterns are embroidered on all parts of the clothing worn by all the ethnic groups. The colours used are usually very strong and stand out very much. Red, blue, pink, purple, white, black and green are usually the most prominent colours used. In the aspect of pattern design the embroidery of the Han ethnic group fully shows the customs while that of the ethnic minorities has the mysterious style of primitive simplicity. The ethnic embroidered clothing, exquisite and ingenious, reflects the skilled embroidery craft of the women of the ethnic minorities. In the aspect of decorative patterns, thanks to the frequent exchange between them, the various ethnic groups, clans and even families use each other's for reference, and supply each other's, thus greatly enriching the varieties, patterns and contents of the embroidery of the various ethnic groups.

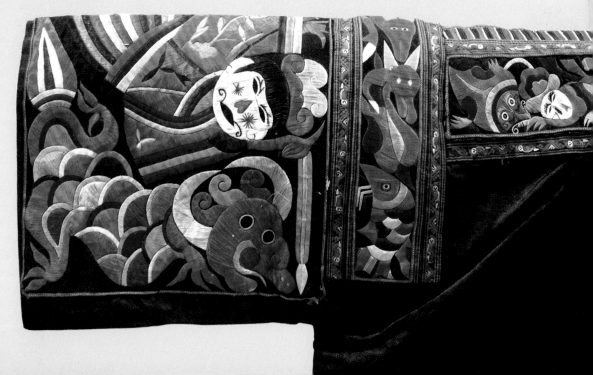

Part of an Embroidered Garment of the Miao Ethnic Group

Featuring a unique ethnic style and artistic craft the embroidered clothing of the Miao ethnic group is famous for its quaint stitching, classic beauty, elegant taste and beautiful colours. This is the sleeve embroidery of an upper outer garment for a girl of the Miao ethnic group.

Part of an Embroidered Garment of the Miao Ethnic Group

This is the sleeve embroidery of an upper outer garment for a girl of the Miao ethnic group. The decorative pattern is "Two Phoenix and a Butterfly Mother" embroidered on a large sleeve.

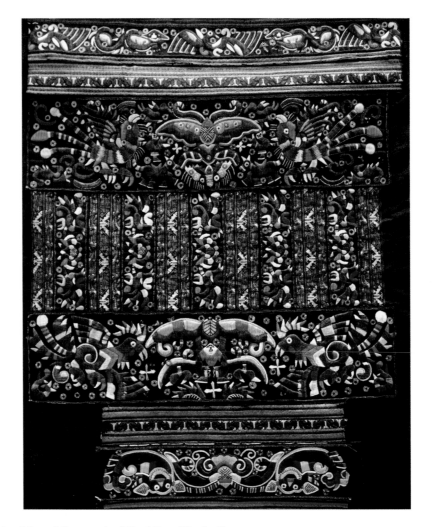

Part of an Embroidered Garment of the Miao Ethnic Group

This is the sleeve embroidery of an upper outer garment for a girl of the Miao ethnic group. The decorative pattern is "Dragon, Phoenix and Butterfly Mother." The people of Miao ethnic group regard the butterfly as their ancestor and respectively call it the "butterfly mother." They embroider it on clothes to show their adoration and respect for their ancestors.

Part of an Embroidered Garment of the Miao Ethnic Group

This embroidery is the part joining the sleeve to the shoulder of an upper outer garment for a girl of the Miao ethnic group. The decorative pattern is "Yang Gong" who is the human ancestor of the Miao ethnic group and who is said to have separated heaven and earth.

An Embroidered Garment of the Miao Ethnic Group

This is an embroidered child's garment. The decorative pattern on the part joining the sleeve and shoulder is "Yang Mei" while that on the cuff is a dragon and that on the middle part of the sleeve is a combination of a phoenix and a butterfly. It takes one to two years to embroider such a splendid garment for a festive or ceremonial occasion.

Part of an Embroidered Garment of the Miao Ethnic Group

This embroidery is part of a child's garment. The decorative pattern on the part joining the sleeve and shoulder is "Yang Gong" and "Yang Mei" and that on the middle part of the sleeve is "Yang Gong Rides a Horse and Yang Mei Rides a Phoenix."

Part of an Embroidered Garment of the Miao Ethnic Group

This embroidery is the sleeve of an upper outer garment for a girl of the Miao ethnic group. The decorative pattern is "Yang Mei," Yang Gong's sister. She is also a human ancestor who is said to have separated heaven and earth in the eyes of Miao ethnic group. It is said that Yang Gong fell in love with his sister actually. Moreover, ignoring the blame and obstacles created by his mother, the God of Heaven and the God of Earth, he finally went through all difficulties and dangers and got married with Yang Mei.

An Embroidered Waistcoat of the Han Ethnic Group

This is an embroidered child's waistcoat. The decorative pattern is a symmetrical lucky peony and a lotus flower, meaning that the offspring shall be prosperous and the family will multiply.

An Embroidered Child's Garment of the Han Ethnic Group

This is an embroidered child's garment with a decorative pattern distributed on the back and sleeve. The pattern on the back is "Children" and that on the left and right is "Guavas" and "Old Deer Standing Close to a Pine Tree" respectively. This implies having both a daughter and a son and they enjoy a long life.

An Embroidered Waistcoat of the Han Ethnic group

This is an embroidered child's waistcoat made from cloth embroidery paste. The cloth embroidery paste is an embroidery technique putting together small pieces of colourful cloth into various patterns. It also called "appliqu." In ancient China there was a folk custom to dress children in a garment made of odd bits of colourful cloth collected from many families so that the children would be protected by many families and be safe. The top part of the decorative pattern is a "Pied Magpie Singing on a Plum Tree" and the bottom is a "Phoenix Amusing Peonies." This implies a wish that the wearer's marriage will be happy and their life prosperous and lucky.

Part of an Embroidered Waistcoat of the Han Ethnic Group

This embroidery is part of a child's waistcoat. The decorative pattern is a segment of a local opera called "Selling Water," which is an excerpt from a traditional opera called Fire Foal. It represents the love story between a young lady Guiying and a child in distress Yangui.

Part of an Embroidered Garment of the Li Ethnic Group

This embroidery is part of an upper outer garment for a girl of the Li ethnic group. The decorative pattern is "The Statue of an Ancestor." The people of the Li ethnic group have a special adoration for their ancestors and embroider their statues on a prominent part of their clothes, which is called "the ancestor worn on clothes."

A Hand Stitched Skirt of the Yao Ethnic Group

This is an embroidered skirt for a girl of the Yao ethnic group. The decorative pattern is "Two Horses Confronting Each Other." The hand stitching of the Yao ethnic group boasts a large variety of complicated designs and patterns with the themes mainly being animals. There is always a picture in a picture and these designs and colours are recognised as the height of perfection.

A Hand Stitched Skirt of the Yao Ethnic Group

    This is an embroidered skirt for a girl of the Yao ethnic group. The decorative pattern is "A Large Lion and a Small Lion" which is a traditional design with an implied meaning. The lion implies officialdom and the whole design symbolizes that official titles pass from generation to generation.

Part of an Embroidered Garment of the Miao Ethnic Group

This embroidery is part of the sleeve of a coat for a girl of the Miao ethnic group. The decorative pattern is a "Centipede Dragon." The combination of a centipede and a dragon is the symbol to eliminate evils and avoid poison.

Folk Hand Stitching

Hand stitching, which is also known as "Shelf Flower" or "Cross Flower", is a traditional style of embroidery stitching which was one of the earliest methods of stitching commonly used. This method of hand stitching features strong regionalism with regard to content and it is most popular in the areas of Hunan, Hubei, central Guizhou, west Guizhou, northwest Guizhou, south Sichuan, Yunnan, northwest Guangxi and Hainan. The decorative patterns used are also the most primitive and they feature a neat style, symmetrical design and are distinctly pointed.

Hand stitching uses a flat cloth and strictly follows the veins of the cloth. It takes the "cross" or "×"shape as the basic stitch, embroidering cross patterns with equal distance and length and arranging them into various designs. When doing hand stitching people first draw the outline with thread and then stitch according to the design at an interval of one yarn or several yarns, which must be in a strict order. Mostly it takes up the thread from the back surface. The patterns are mostly of a geometrical design often combining several small flowers with a big one and surrounded by diamond panes. It can take up the thread from the front surface or the back surface but both must be appreciated from the front surface. The stitching of the former one is easy to learn and is the most popular one used and the stitching of the latter one needs to be practiced for a long time. The latter one is to be found only in specific regions.

These hand stitching embroideries are mostly done on everyday items such as clothes, handkerchiefs, headbands, aprons, portieres and curtains. In the layout of "hand stitching," there is usually a large group of flowers in the centre of the cloth and a continuous double-pattern composition in the four corners similar to a brocade design. The pattern in the centre mostly uses octagonal, diamond, crisscross and square shapes with varying repeated designs piled up. The designs are usually geometrical figures or groups of flowers which are the combination of several bouquets of flowers formed by many basic designs. All the designs are symmetrical. There are many basic designs with fairly complicated procedures. With regard to the patterns they vary in their density and their degree of complication.

A Hand Stitched Rectangular Cloth

The designs of the embossed embroidery found in Hunan Province are mostly traditional good luck ones. The most common ones are "Carp Jumping Over the Dragon Door," "Magpies Standing on a Plum Tree" and "Two Dragons Playing With a Ball" and they also have complicated characters from myths and dramas. The design in the centre of this embroidery is a folk story entitled "The Mice Getting Their Daughter Married."

Part of a Huaxi Hand-Stitched Hebao Bag

　　The designs of the Huaxi Miao hand stitching usually use either a symmetrical continual double-pattern or a quadruple-pattern composition or a single pattern. The colours are mainly white, red, yellow, pink and green, rarely using other colours. The design of this embroidery is a combination of a spiny pear flower and a butterfly flower.

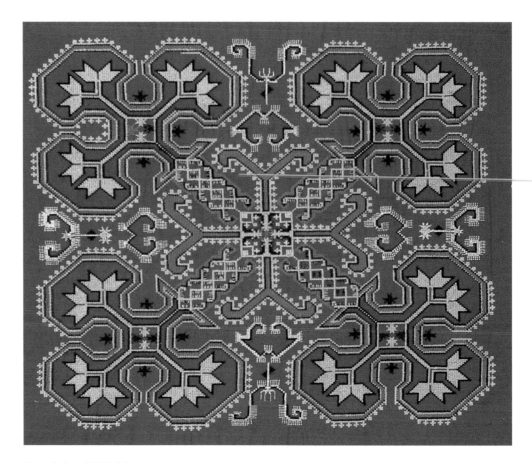

Huaxi Hand Stitching

As it is restricted by the cross stitch cross hand stitching has to be very precise. The designs of this style of stitching are very functional and decorative. The design of this particular embroidery is a combination of a butterfly flower and a maple tree. The maple tree is one of the totems worshiped by the people of Miao ethnic group.

Huaxi Hand Stitching

The Huaxi Miao ethnic group, in order not to dirty the embroidery in the course of an embossed embroidery, take up a single silk thread or blend one from the back surface, forming an artistic style of "embroidering from the back surface and appreciating it from the front." This embroidery design is a butterfly flower which varies in the combination of the butterfly and the flowers.

A Hand-Stitched Apron

This particular embroidery is a hand stitched apron coming from an area of Hubei Province. The designs used in Hubei Province are mainly traditional good luck ones such as "Birds Adoring the Phoenix," "Two Fish Amusing Themselves in the Water" and "Golden Melon and Peony."

A Hand-Stitched Face Cloth

This embroidery is a hand stitched face cloth coming from an area of Hubei Province and is commonly used as a family decoration. The design is a traditional one, "Birds Adoring the Phoenix," and is done around some good luck characters in the centre.